★★★★★★ AMERICA COOKS ★★★★★★

northwest flavors

★★★★★★ AMERICA COOKS ★★★★★★

northwest flavors

an all-american taste of the mountains, woods and waters

lindley boegehold

southwater

This edition is published by Southwater

Southwater is an imprint of Anness Publishing Ltd, Hermes House, 88–89 Blackfriars Road, London SE1 8HA
tel. 020 7401 2077; fax 020 7633 9499 www.southwaterbooks.com; info@anness.com

Published in the USA by Southwater
Anness Publishing Inc
fax 212 807 6813

Distributed in the UK by The Manning Partnership
tel. 01225 852 727; fax 01225 852 852
sales@manning-partnership.co.uk

Distributed in the USA by National Book Network
tel. 301 459 3366; fax 301 459 1705
www.nbnbooks.com

Distributed in Canada by General Publishing
tel. 416 445 3333; fax 416 445 5991
www.genpub.com

Distributed in Australia by Sandstone Publishing
tel. 02 9560 7888; fax 02 9560 7488
sales@sandstonepublishing.com.au

Distributed in New Zealand by
The Five Mile Press (NZ) Ltd
tel. (09) 444 4144; fax (09) 444 4518; fivemilenz@clear.net.nz

A CIP catalogue record for this book is available from the British Library.

Publisher: Joanna Lorenz
Managing Editor: Helen Sudell
Designer: Nigel Partridge
Photographer: Amanda Haywood and Ken Graham, Picture Perfect, USA (p 6/7)
Illustrations by: Estelle Corke
Recipes by: Carla Capalbo and Laura Washburn

Front cover shows Wild Rice – for recipe, see p 49

Previously published as *Recipes from the Pacific Northwest*

1 3 5 7 9 10 8 6 4 2

NOTES

Standard spoon and cup measures are level.
Large eggs are used unless otherwise stated.

Contents

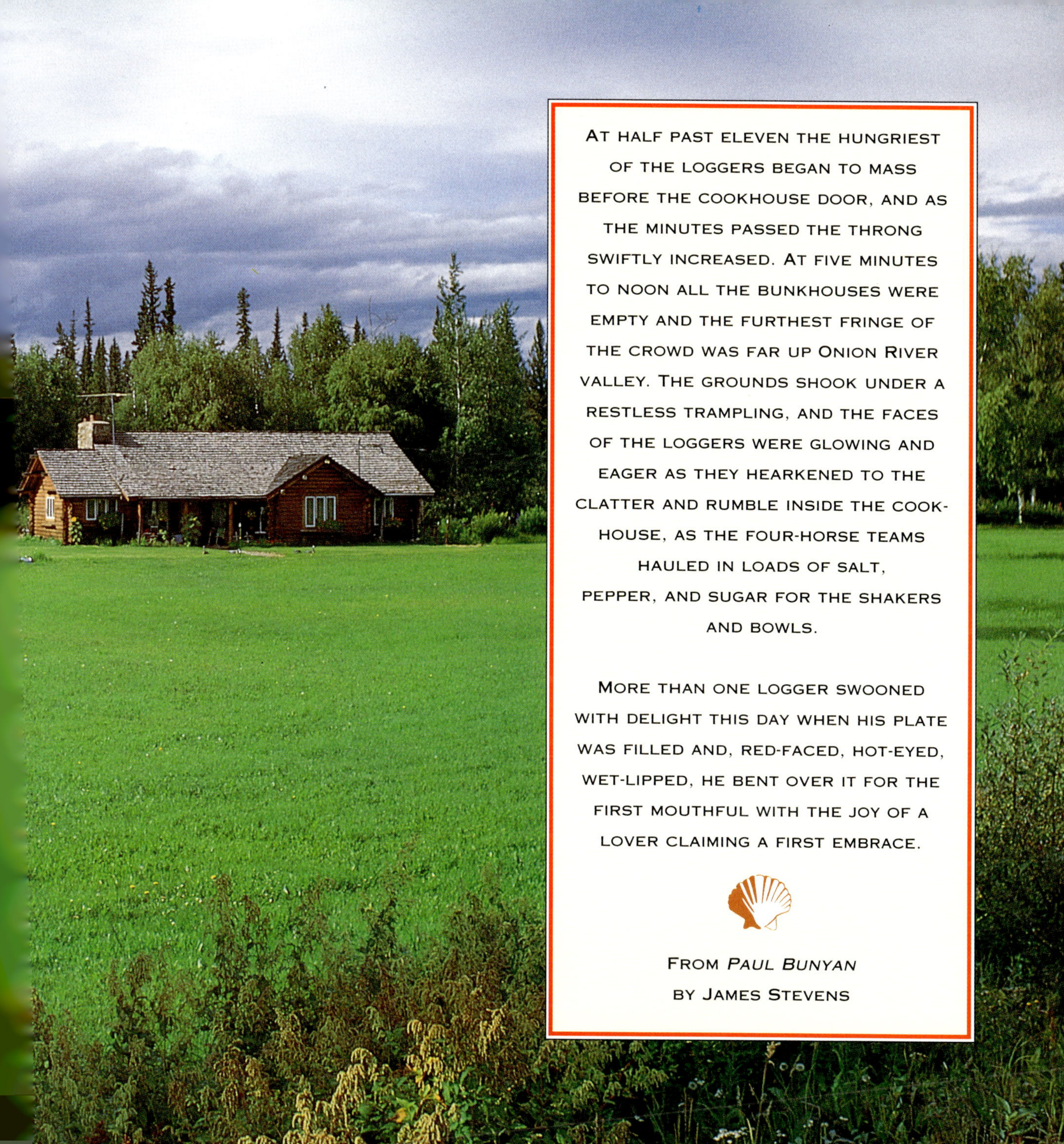

At half past eleven the hungriest of the loggers began to mass before the cookhouse door, and as the minutes passed the throng swiftly increased. At five minutes to noon all the bunkhouses were empty and the furthest fringe of the crowd was far up Onion River valley. The grounds shook under a restless trampling, and the faces of the loggers were glowing and eager as they hearkened to the clatter and rumble inside the cookhouse, as the four-horse teams hauled in loads of salt, pepper, and sugar for the shakers and bowls.

More than one logger swooned with delight this day when his plate was filled and, red-faced, hot-eyed, wet-lipped, he bent over it for the first mouthful with the joy of a lover claiming a first embrace.

From *Paul Bunyan*
by James Stevens

SMOKED TURKEY AND LENTIL SOUP

THE SMOKINESS OF THE TURKEY GIVES A UNIQUE FLAVOR TO THIS HEARTY SOUP. SMOKED CHICKEN OR HAM WORKS EQUALLY WELL.

SERVES 4

2 tablespoons butter
1 large carrot, chopped
1 onion, chopped
1 celery stalk, chopped
1 leek, white part only, chopped
4 ounces mushrooms, chopped
¼ cup dry white wine
4½ cups chicken stock
2 teaspoons dried thyme
1 bay leaf
½ cup lentils
8 ounces smoked turkey meat, diced
salt and pepper
chopped fresh parsley, for garnishing

Melt the butter in a large saucepan. Add the carrot, onion, leek, celery, and mushrooms. Cook until golden, 3-5 minutes.

Stir in the wine and chicken stock. Bring to a boil and skim off with a spoon any foam that rises to the surface. Add the thyme and bay leaf. Lower the heat, cover, and simmer gently 30 minutes.

Add the lentils and continue cooking, covered, until they are just tender, 30-40 minutes more (see above). Stir the soup from time to time.

Stir in the turkey and season to taste with salt and pepper. Cook until just heated through. Ladle into bowls and garnish with parsley.

Serve hot with white crusty bread.

VARIATION

FOR A MORE SUBSTANTIAL SOUP, ADD ABOUT 1 CUP OF FINELY CHOPPED HAM FOR THE LAST TEN MINUTES OF COOKING TIME.

SALMON CHOWDER

THIS RICH AND ELEGANT SOUP IS A MEAL IN ITSELF. SERVE IT WITH SPINACH SALAD AND A GLASS OF CHARDONNAY.

SERVES 4

1½ tablespoons butter or margarine
1 onion, minced
1 leek, minced
½ cup minced fennel bulb
¼ cup flour
1½ quarts fish stock
2 cups potatoes, cut in ½ inch cubes (about 2 medium-size potatoes)
salt and pepper
1 pound boneless, skinless salmon, cut in ¾ inch cubes
¾ cup milk
½ cup whipping cream
2 tablespoons chopped fresh dill

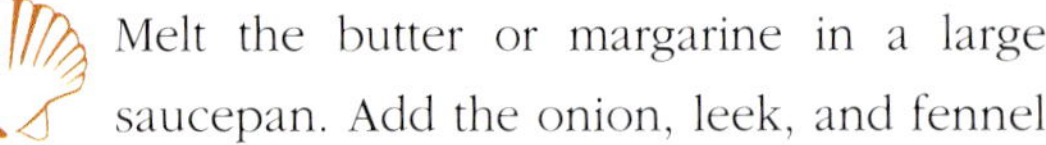

Melt the butter or margarine in a large saucepan. Add the onion, leek, and fennel and cook over medium heat until softened, 5-8 minutes, stirring occasionally.

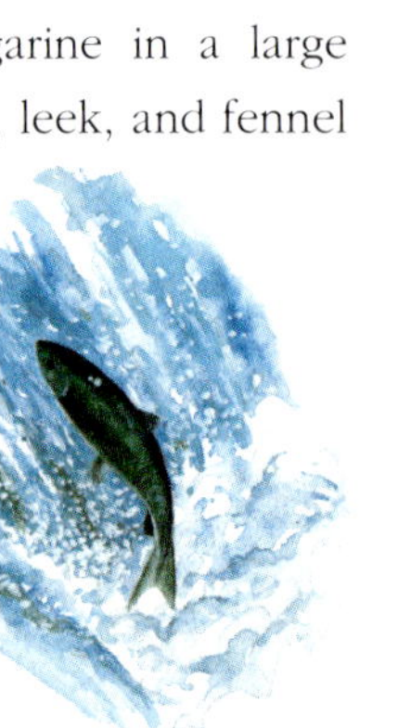

Stir in the flour. Reduce the heat to low and cook, stirring occasionally, for approximately 3 minutes.

Add the stock and potatoes. Season with salt and pepper to taste. Bring to a boil, then reduce the heat, cover, and simmer until the potatoes are tender, about 20 minutes.

Add the salmon and simmer until just cooked, about 3-5 minutes.

Stir in the milk, cream, and dill. Cook just until warmed through; do not boil. Taste and adjust the seasoning, if necessary, then serve.

TOMATO-BLUE CHEESE SOUP WITH BACON

OREGON IS KNOWN FOR DELICIOUS CHEESES THAT ARE PRODUCED BY DAIRY FARMERS ACROSS THE STATE. THIS PUNGENT SOUP USES A NATIVE BLUE CHEESE THAT COMPLEMENTS THE SWEETNESS OF THE TOMATOES.

SERVES 4

3 pounds ripe tomatoes, peeled, quartered, and seeded
2 garlic cloves, minced
salt and pepper
2 tablespoons vegetable oil or butter
1 leek, chopped
1 carrot, chopped
1 quart unsalted chicken stock
4 ounces Oregon Blue Cheese, crumbled
3 tablespoons whipping cream
several large fresh basil leaves, or 1-2 fresh parsley sprigs
6 ounces bacon, cooked and crumbled

Preheat the oven to 400°F. Spread the tomatoes in a baking dish. Sprinkle with the garlic and some salt and pepper. Place in the oven and bake 35 minutes.

Heat the oil or butter in a large saucepan. Add the chopped leek and carrot and season lightly with salt and pepper to taste. Cook over low heat, stirring often, until softened, about 10 minutes.

Stir in the stock and tomatoes. Bring to a boil, then lower the heat, cover, and simmer 20 minutes.

Add the blue cheese, cream and basil or parsley. Transfer to a food processor or blender and process until smooth (work in batches if necessary). Taste for seasoning.

If necessary, reheat the soup, but do not boil. Ladle into bowls and sprinkle with crumbled bacon.

Macaroni and Blue Cheese

This comforting supper dish is given a tangy twist with blue cheese instead of the usual cheddar.

Serves 6

1 pound macaroni
1 quart milk
4 tablespoons butter
6 tablespoons flour
¼ teaspoon salt
8 ounces Oregon Blue Cheese, crumbled
black pepper, for serving

Preheat the oven to 350°F. Grease a 13- x 9-inch baking dish.

Bring a large pot of water to a boil. Salt to taste and add the macaroni. Cook until just tender (check package directions for cooking times). Drain and rinse under cold water. Place in a large bowl. Set aside.

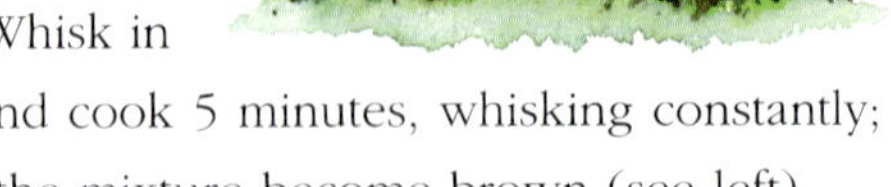

In another pan, bring the milk to a boil and set aside.

Melt the butter in a heavy saucepan over low heat. Whisk in the flour and cook 5 minutes, whisking constantly; do not let the mixture become brown (see left).

Remove from the heat and whisk the hot milk into the butter and flour mixture. When the mixture is smoothly blended, return to medium heat and continue cooking, whisking constantly, until the sauce is thick, about 5 minutes. Add the salt.

Add the sauce to the macaroni. Add three-quarters of the crumbled blue cheese and stir well. Transfer the macaroni mixture to the prepared baking dish and spread in an even layer.

Sprinkle the remaining cheese evenly over the surface. Bake until bubbling hot, about 25 minutes.

If desired, lightly brown the top of the macaroni and cheese under the broiler, 3-4 minutes. Serve hot, sprinkled with freshly ground black pepper.

SEATTLE FISH FRITTERS

THIS RECIPE RELIES ON THE BOUNTEOUS CROP OF SEAFOOD AVAILABLE IN FISH MARKETS ALONG THE COAST. YOU CAN VARY THE TYPES OF FISH AND SHELLFISH DEPENDING ON WHAT IS FRESH AND AVAILABLE.

SERVES 4

½ fennel bulb, cut in pieces
1 medium leek, cut in pieces
1 green bell pepper, seeded and cut in pieces
2 garlic cloves
1 tablespoon butter
⅛ teaspoon red pepper flakes
salt and pepper
6 ounces skinless boneless salmon, cut in pieces
3½ ounces skinless boneless ling cod or rockfish, cut in pieces
3 ounces cooked peeled shrimp
1 cup flour
6 eggs, beaten
1½-2 cups milk
1 tablespoon chopped fresh basil
4-6 tablespoons oil, for greasing
sour cream, for serving

Combine the fennel, leek, bell pepper, and garlic in a food processor or blender and process until finely chopped.

Melt the butter in a skillet until sizzling. Add the vegetable mixture and red pepper flakes. Season with salt and pepper. Cook the mixture over a low heat until softened, about 8-10 minutes. Remove from the heat and set aside.

Combine the salmon, ling cod or rockfish, and shrimp in the food processor or blender. Process, using the pulse button and scraping the sides of the container several times, until the mixture is coarsely chopped. Scrape into a large bowl and set aside.

Sift the flour into another bowl and make a well in the center.

Gradually whisk in the eggs alternately with 1½ cups milk to make a smooth batter. If necessary, strain the batter to remove lumps.

Stir the seafood, vegetables, and basil into the batter. If it seems too thick, add some more milk a little at a time.

Lightly oil a griddle or nonstick skillet and heat over medium heat. Spoon in the batter by ⅓ cupfuls. Cook until the fritters are golden around the edges, 2-3 minutes. Turn them over and cook the other side, 2-3 minutes more. Work in batches, keeping the cooked fritters warm.

Serve hot, with sour cream.

Scalloped Oysters

EXPERIENCE CULTIVATED OYSTERS AT THEIR BEST; FROM THE COPPERY TASTING BELUNS TO MALPEQUES, KENT ISLAND AND CANADIAN GOLDEN MANTLES. THEY ALL TASTE GOOD IN THIS CLASSIC PREPARATION.

SERVES 4

7 tablespoons butter
1 shallot, minced
4 ounces mushrooms, minced
½ teaspoon flour
⅛ teaspoon hot pepper sauce
salt and pepper
24 oysters, shucked and drained
⅓ cup dry white wine
⅔ cup whipping cream
2 tablespoons chopped fresh parsley
6 tablespoons fresh bread crumbs

Preheat the oven to 375°F. Grease a 6- x 8-inch baking dish.

Melt the butter in a skillet. Add the shallot and mushrooms and cook until softened, 3 minutes.

Add the flour and hot pepper sauce. Season with salt and pepper. Cook, stirring constantly, 1 minute.

Stir in the oysters and wine, scraping the bottom of the skillet. Add the cream (see above right). Transfer the mixture to the prepared baking dish.

In a small bowl, combine the chopped parsley, fresh bread crumbs, and salt to taste. Stir to mix.

Sprinkle the crumbs evenly over the oyster mixture. Bake until the top is golden and the sauce bubbling, 15-20 minutes. Serve immediately.

COOK'S TIP

IF YOU HAVE BOUGHT OYSTERS STILL IN THEIR SHELLS, YOU CAN SHUCK THEM BY PUSHING IN THE POINT OF AN OYSTER KNIFE ABOUT ½ INCH INTO THE HINGE. PUSH DOWN FIRMLY AND THE LID SHOULD POP OPEN.

PENN COVE STEAMED MUSSELS

THE SLIGHT FLAVOR OF ANISE OF FENNEL GIVES THE MUSSELS A SOPHISTICATED FLAVOR. SERVE WITH LOTS OF CRUSTY BREAD TO SOP UP THE SAUCE.

SERVES 2

1½ pounds mussels in shell
½ fennel bulb, minced
1 shallot, minced
3 tablespoons dry white wine
3 tablespoons whipping cream
2 tablespoons chopped fresh parsley
black pepper

Scrub the mussels under cold running water. Remove barnacles with a small knife, and remove the beards (see below). Rinse.

Place the mussels in a large skillet with a lid.

Sprinkle them with the fennel, shallot, and wine. Cover the skillet and place over medium-high heat. Steam until the mussels open, 3-5 minutes.

Lift out the mussels with a slotted spoon and remove the top shells. Discard any mussels that did not open. Arrange the mussels, on their bottom shells, in one layer in a shallow serving dish. Keep warm.

Place a double layer of dampened cheesecloth in a strainer set over a bowl. Strain the mussel cooking liquid through the cheesecloth. Return the liquid to a clean saucepan and bring to a boil.

Add the cream, stir well, and boil 3 minutes to reduce slightly. Stir in the parsley. Spoon the sauce over the mussels and sprinkle with freshly ground black pepper. Serve the mussels immediately.

COOK'S TIP

ALWAYS CHOOSE THE FRESHEST MUSSELS FOR COOKING, AND DO NOT ATTEMPT TO PREPARE THEM MORE THAN A FEW HOURS IN ADVANCE OF COOKING AS MUSSELLS SOON SPOIL AND DIE.

PASTA WITH SCALLOPS

IF YOU HAVE A CHANCE, TAKE A TRIP TO PIKE'S PLACE FARMER'S MARKET IN SEATTLE WHERE THEY WILL SHUCK THE SCALLOPS RIGHT IN FRONT OF YOU.

SERVES 4

1 pound pasta, such as fettucine or linguine
2 tablespoons olive oil
2 garlic cloves, minced
1 pound sea scallops, sliced in half horizontally
salt and pepper

FOR THE SAUCE

2 tablespoons olive oil
½ onion, minced
1 garlic clove, minced
½ teaspoon salt
1 28 - ounce can peeled tomatoes
2 tablespoons chopped fresh basil.

For the sauce, heat the oil in a nonstick skillet. Add the onion, garlic, and a little salt, and cook over medium heat until just softened, about 5 minutes, stirring occasionally.

Add the tomatoes, with their juice, and crush with the tines of a fork. Bring quickly to a boil, then reduce the heat, and simmer gently for 15 minutes. Remove from the heat and set aside.

Bring a large pot of salted water to a boil. Add the pasta and cook until just tender to the bite (check package directions for timing).

Meanwhile, combine the oil and garlic in another nonstick skillet and cook until just sizzling, about 30 seconds. Add the scallops and ½ teaspoon salt and cook over high heat, tossing, until the scallops are cooked through, about 3 minutes.

Add the scallops to the tomato sauce. Season with salt and pepper, stir, and keep warm.

Drain the pasta, rinse under hot water, and drain again. Place in a large warmed serving bowl. Add the scallop sauce and the basil and toss thoroughly. Serve immediately.

COOK'S TIP

IF POSSIBLE, ASK YOUR FISHMONGER TO SAVE YOU THE ROE. IT IS A SAVORY PART OF THE SCALLOP THAT IS USUALLY DISCARDED BY FISHERMEN.

Clam and Sausage Chili

This hearty dish combines the fruits of the sea and land. Accompany it with a cold beer such as Anchor Steam, from one of the region's many microbreweries.

Serves 4

1 cup dried black beans, soaked overnight and drained
1 bay leaf
2 teaspoons coarse salt
½ pound lean bulk pork sausage meat
1 tablespoon vegetable oil
1 onion, minced
1 garlic clove, minced
1 teaspoon fennel seeds
1 teaspoon dried oregano
¼ teaspoon red pepper flakes, or to taste
2-3 teaspoons chili powder, or to taste
1 teaspoon ground cumin
2 16-ounce cans chopped tomatoes in purée
½ cup dry white wine
1½ cups drained canned clams (approximately 2 10-ounce cans), liquid reserved
salt and pepper

Put the beans in a large pot. Add fresh cold water to cover and the bay leaf. Bring to a boil, then cover, and simmer 30 minutes. Add the coarse salt and continue simmering until tender, about 30 minutes more. Drain and discard bay leaf.

Put the sausage meat in a large flameproof casserole. Cook over medium heat until just beginning to brown, 2-3 minutes. Stir frequently to break up lumps. Add the oil, onion and garlic.

Continue cooking until the vegetables are softened, about 5 minutes more, stirring occasionally.

Stir in the herbs and spices, tomatoes, wine, and ⅔ cup of the reserved clam juice. Bring to a boil, then lower the heat and cook, stirring occasionally, 15 minutes.

Add the black beans and clams and stir to combine (see above). Taste and adjust the seasoning if necessary. Continue cooking just until the clams are heated through. Serve immediately.

Pan-Fried Trout with Horseradish Sauce

This dish tastes best when just-caught trout is gutted and fried over a camp fire after a fruitful day of fishing, but it is also easy to eat in a dining room.

Serves 4

4 whole rainbow trout, about 6 ounces each, cleaned
salt and pepper
¼ cup flour
2 tablespoons butter
1 tablespoon vegetable oil

For the sauce

½ cup mayonnaise
½ cup sour cream
¾ teaspoon grated horseradish
¼ teaspoon paprika
2 tablespoons tomato or lemon juice
1 tablespoon chopped fresh herbs, such as chives, parsley, or basil

For the sauce, combine the mayonnaise, sour cream, horseradish, paprika, tomato or lemon juice, and herbs. Season with salt and pepper and mix well. Set the sauce aside.

Rinse the trout and pat dry. Season the cavities in the fish generously with salt and pepper.

Combine the flour, ½ teaspoon salt, and a little pepper in a shallow dish. Fully coat the trout on both sides with the seasoned flour, shaking off any excess.

Heat the butter and oil in a large nonstick skillet over medium-high heat. When sizzling, add the trout and cook until opaque throughout, approximately 4-5 minutes on each side (see above).

Serve immediately, with the sauce.

Variation

If rainbow trout is unavailable, try a small salmon trout – it tastes every bit as good.

SALMON WITH SIZZLING HERBS

THE EXOTIC ORIENTAL FLAVORS OF GINGER, SCALLION AND CILANTRO PERFECTLY ACCENT THE RICHNESS OF THE SALMON.

SERVES 4

4 salmon steaks, 6-7 ounces each
salt and pepper
⅓ cup olive oil
½ cup chopped fresh cilantro
3 tablespoons minced fresh gingerroot
½ cup chopped scallions
¼ cup soy sauce, plus extra for serving

Bring some water (about 1-2 inches) to a boil in the bottom of a steamer.

Season well the fish steaks on both sides with salt and pepper.

Place the fish steaks in the top part of the steamer. Cover the pan and steam until the fish is opaque throughout, 7-8 minutes.

Meanwhile, heat the oil in a small heavy saucepan until very hot. (To test the temperature, drop in a piece of chopped scallion; if it sizzles, the oil is hot enough.)

Place the steamed salmon steaks on plates that have been warmed through.

Divide the chopped cilantro among the salmon steaks, mounding it on top of the fish. Sprinkle with the ginger and then the scallions (see left). Drizzle 1 tablespoon of soy sauce over each salmon steak.

Spoon the hot oil over each salmon steak and serve immediately, with additional soy sauce.

COOK'S TIP

SERVE RICE ON THE SIDE, TO SOAK UP THE DELICIOUS JUICES, AND A GREEN SALAD.

Seattle Chicken Wings

These light and spicy wings are irresistible. A squeeze of fresh lime before serving gives them extra sparkle.

Serves 4

⅓ cup soy sauce
1 tablespoon light brown sugar
1 tablespoon rice vinegar
2 tablespoons dry sherry wine
juice of 1 orange
2-inch strip of orange peel
1 star anise
1 teaspoon cornstarch
¼ cup water
1 tablespoon minced fresh ginger root
¼-1 teaspoon Oriental chili-garlic sauce, to taste
3½ pounds chicken wings (22-24), tips removed

Preheat the oven to 400°F.

Combine the soy sauce, brown sugar, vinegar, sherry wine, orange juice and peel, and star anise in a saucepan. Slowly bring to a boil over medium heat.

Combine the cornstarch and water in a small bowl and stir until blended. Add to the boiling soy sauce mixture, stirring well. Boil 1 minute more, stirring constantly.

Remove the soy sauce mixture from the heat and stir in the minced ginger and chili-garlic sauce.

Arrange the chicken wings, in one layer, in a large baking dish. Pour over the soy sauce mixture and stir to coat the wings evenly (see above).

Bake until tender and browned, 30-40 minutes, basting occasionally. Serve the wings hot or warm.

Variation

For a spicy fish dish, substitute 4 catfish fillets for the chicken. Do not slice them in half, but season as chicken and cook 2 minutes on the first side and 1½ minutes on the other side.

Lemon Chicken with Guacamole Sauce

If you can cook this whole meal outside on the grill, so much the better. Try to find Hass avocados for the sauce. They have bumpy blackish skins and have creamier, richer flesh than the larger, bright green, smooth-skinned ones.

Serves 4

juice of 2 lemons
3 tablespoons olive oil
2 garlic cloves, minced
salt and pepper
4 chicken breasts, about 7 ounces each
2 beefsteak tomatoes, cored and cut in half
chopped fresh cilantro, for garnishing

For the sauce

1 ripe avocado
¼ cup sour cream
3 tablespoons fresh lemon juice
½ teaspoon salt
¼ cup water

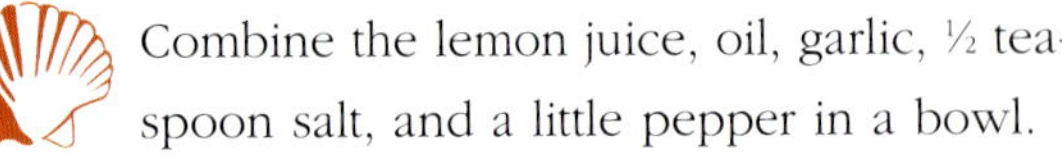

Combine the lemon juice, oil, garlic, ½ teaspoon salt, and a little pepper in a bowl.

Arrange the chicken breasts, in one layer, in a shallow glass or ceramic dish. Pour over the lemon mixture and coat evenly. Cover and let stand for 1 hour at room temperature, or refrigerate overnight.

For the sauce, cut the avocado in half, remove the pit, and scrape the flesh into a food processor.

Add the sour cream, lemon juice, and salt and process until smooth. Add the water and process just to blend. If necessary, add more water to thin the sauce. Transfer to a bowl, taste and adjust the seasoning, if necessary. Set aside.

Preheat the broiler. Heat a ridged grill pan. Remove the chicken from the marinade and pat dry.

When the grill pan is hot, add the chicken breasts and cook, turning often, until they are cooked through, about 10 minutes.

Meanwhile, arrange the tomato halves, cut-sides up, on a baking sheet and season lightly with salt and pepper. Broil until bubbling, about 5 minutes.

To serve, place a chicken breast, tomato half, and a dollop of avocado sauce on each plate. Sprinkle with coriander and serve.

Variation

To grill the chicken, prepare the fire, and when the coals are glowing red and covered with grey ash, spread them in a single layer. Set an oiled grill rack about 5 inches above the coals and cook the chicken breasts until lightly charred and cooked through, about 15-20 minutes. Allow extra olive oil for basting.

CHICKEN-MUSHROOM PIE

DRIED WILD MUSHROOMS GIVE THIS PIE ITS WOODSY FLAVOR. FOR AN EVEN MORE INTENSE TASTE, USE FRESH CREMINI OR PORCINI MUSHROOMS AS WELL AS THE DRIED.

SERVES 6

½ ounce dried porcini mushrooms
4 tablespoons butter
2 tablespoons flour
1 cup chicken stock, warmed
¼ cup whipping cream or milk
salt and pepper
1 onion, coarsely chopped
2 carrots, sliced
2 celery stalks, coarsely chopped
2 ounces fresh mushrooms, quartered
1 pound cooked chicken meat, cubed
½ cup shelled fresh or frozen peas
beaten egg, for glazing

FOR THE CRUST

2 cups flour
¼ teaspoon salt
½ cup (1 stick) cold butter, cut in pieces
⅓ cup shortening
4-8 tablespoons ice water

For the crust, sift the flour and salt into a bowl. With a pastry blender or 2 knives, cut in the butter and shortening until the mixture resembles coarse meal. Sprinkle with 6 tablespoons ice water and mix until the dough holds together. If the dough is too crumbly, add a little more water, 1 tablespoon at a time. Gather the dough into a ball and flatten into a disk. Wrap in wax paper and refrigerate at least 30 minutes.

Place the porcini mushrooms in a small bowl. Add hot water to cover and soak until soft, about 30 minutes. Lift out of the water with a slotted spoon to leave any grit behind and drain.

Preheat the oven to 375°F.

Melt 2 tablespoons of the butter in a heavy saucepan. Whisk in the flour and cook until bubbling, whisking constantly. Add the warm stock and cook over medium heat, whisking, until the mixture boils. Cook 2-3 minutes more. Whisk in the cream or milk. Season with salt and pepper. Set aside.

Heat the remaining butter in a large nonstick skillet until foamy. Add the onion and carrots and cook until softened, about 5 minutes. Add the celery and fresh mushrooms and cook 5 minutes more. Stir in the chicken, peas, and porcini mushrooms.

Add the chicken mixture to the cream sauce and stir to mix. Taste for seasoning. Transfer to a 10-cup rectangular baking dish.

Roll out the dough to about ⅛ inch thickness. Cut out a rectangle about 1 inch larger all around than the dish. Lay the dough over the filling. Make a decorative edge by crimping the dough at the edge.

Cut several vents in the top crust to allow steam to escape. Brush with the egg glaze.

Press together the dough trimmings, then roll out again. Cut into strips and lay them over the top crust. Glaze again. If desired, roll small balls of dough and set them in the "windows" in the lattice.

Bake until the top crust is browned, about 30 minutes. Serve the pie hot from the dish.

Pork Chops with Cider and Apples

THIS RECIPE HEADS INLAND TO THE FARMS AND ORCHARDS. PREPARE IT IN THE FALL WHEN FRESH CIDER IS AVAILABLE.

SERVES 4

1 pound tart cooking apples (3-4), peeled, quartered, and cored
4 pork chops, about 1 inch thick
1 teaspoon dried thyme
¼ teaspoon ground allspice
salt and pepper
1 tablespoon butter
1 tablespoon vegetable oil
1 bay leaf
½ cup apple cider
2 tablespoons whipping cream
potato pancakes, for serving

Preheat the oven to 375°F. Grease a casserole large enough to hold the pork chops in one layer.

Spread the apples in an even layer in the prepared dish. Set aside.

Sprinkle the pork chops on both sides with the thyme, ground allspice, and a little salt and pepper.

Heat the butter and oil in a skillet. When hot, add the pork chops and cook over medium-high heat until browned, 2-3 minutes. Turn around and cook the other side, for a further 2-3 minutes. Remove from the heat.

Arrange the pork chops on top of the apples (see above). Add the bay leaf and pour over the cider. Cover and bake for 15 minutes.

Turn the chops over. Continue baking until they are cooked through, about 15 minutes more.

Transfer the pork chops to warmed plates. Remove the apple quarters with a slotted spoon and divide them among the plates.

Stir the cream into the sauce and heat just until warmed through. Taste for seasoning. Spoon the sauce over the pork chops and serve immediately with potato pancakes.

Pork Braised in Beer

USE A FULL-FLAVORED BEER OR ALE IN THIS DISH. THE NORTHWEST'S MANY MICROBREWERIES OFFER A WIDE RANGE OF DELICIOUS INDIVIDUAL VARIETIES.

SERVES 6

4-5 pound loin of pork, boned, trimmed of excess fat, and tied into a neat shape
salt and pepper
1 tablespoon butter
1 tablespoon vegetable oil
3 large onions, halved and thinly sliced
1 garlic clove, minced
3 cups beer
1 bay leaf
1 tablespoon flour blended with 2 tablespoons water

Season the pork roast on all sides with salt and pepper. Heat the butter and oil in a flameproof casserole just large enough to hold the pork loin. When hot, add the roast and brown on all sides, 5-7 minutes, turning it to color evenly. Remove from the pot and set aside.

Drain excess fat from the pot, leaving about 1 tablespoon. Add the onions and garlic and cook just until softened, about 5 minutes.

Stir in the beer (see left), scraping to remove any bits on the bottom of the pan. Add the bay leaf.

Return the pork roast to the casserole. Cover and slowly cook over low heat about 2 hours, turning the roast over about halfway through the cooking time.

Remove the pork roast. Cut it into serving slices and arrange on a platter. Cover and keep warm.

Discard the bay leaf. Add the flour to the cooking juices and cook over high heat, stirring constantly, until thickened. Taste for seasoning. Pour the sauce over the pork slices.

Serve immediately with a crisp green salad.

Oregon Blue Cheese Burgers

Blue cheese gives new life to the traditional cheese burger. Top with sauteed mushrooms for an even more ecstatic eating experience.

Serves 4

2 pounds lean ground beef
1 garlic clove, minced
2 tablespoons chopped fresh parsley
2 tablespoons chopped fresh chives
½ teaspoon salt
pepper
8 ounces Oregon Blue Cheese, crumbled
4 hamburger buns, split and toasted
tomato slices and lettuce, for serving
mustard or catsup, for serving

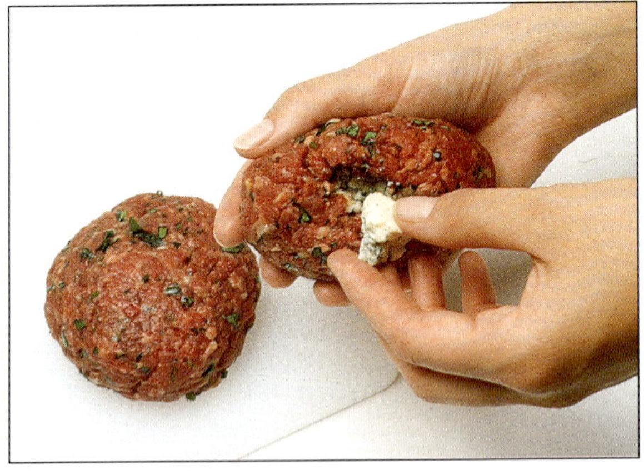

In a bowl, combine the beef, garlic, parsley, chives, salt, and a little pepper. Mix together, and form into 4 thick patties.

Make a slit in the side of each patty, poking well into the beef to form a pocket. Fill each pocket with 2 ounces of the blue cheese (see above right).

Close the holes to seal the blue cheese inside the patties.

Heat a ridged grill pan (or preheat the broiler). Cook the burgers 4-5 minutes on each side for medium-rare, 6-7 minutes for well-done.

Place the burgers in the split hamburger buns. Serve immediately, with sliced tomatoes and lettuce leaves, and mustard or catsup if desired.

Cook's Tip

If cooking time is short, these cheese burgers can be prepared the day before and refrigerated overnight. They are also excellent cooked on a barbecue - serve with ice cold beers.

Steak with Mushrooms and Leeks in Red Wine

Use a variety of mushrooms — porcini, cremini or the magnificent morels — to accent the hearty taste of beef, and serve with an Oregon Pinot Noir, if possible.

Serves 4

6-8 leeks (about 1¼ pounds), white and light green parts only

¼ cup olive oil

1½ pounds mushrooms, quartered

2 cups dry red wine, such as an Oregon Pinot Noir or a Washington State Merlot

salt and pepper

4 8-ounce boneless sirloin steaks, about ¾ inch thick

1 tablespoon chopped fresh parsley

With a sharp knife, trim the leeks and cut into 1-inch slices on the diagonal.

Heat 3 tablespoons of the oil in a large skillet. When hot, add the leeks and mushrooms and cook over medium heat, until lightly browned (see above right).

Stir in the wine, scraping the bottom of the pan. Season with salt and pepper. Bring to a boil and boil 1 minute. Reduce the heat to low, then cover and cook 5 minutes.

Remove the lid, raise the heat, and cook until the wine has reduced slightly, 5 minutes. Set aside.

Brush the steaks with the remaining 1 tablespoon oil and sprinkle generously on both sides with salt and pepper.

Heat a ridged grill pan (or preheat the broiler). When hot, add the steaks and cook 3-4 minutes on each side for medium-rare.

Meanwhile, stir the parsley into the leek mixture and reheat.

Place the steaks on 4 warmed plates. Mound the leek mixture on top and serve.

Variation

When in season, fresh wild mushrooms add that extra flavor to this wholesome dish.

Smoked Trout Pasta Salad

IF YOU DON'T HAPPEN TO BE A RUGGED FISHERMAN WHO CATCHES AND SMOKES YOUR OWN FISH YOU CAN BUY DELICIOUS SMOKED TROUT AT MOST DELICATESSENS AND GOURMET FOOD STORES.

SERVES 6

1 tablespoon butter
1 cup minced bulb fennel
6 scallions, 2 minced and 4 thinly sliced
salt and pepper
8 ounces skinless smoked trout fillets, flaked
3 tablespoons chopped fresh dill
½ cup mayonnaise
2 teaspoons fresh lemon juice
2 tablespoons whipping cream
1 pound small pasta shapes, such as shells
fresh dill sprigs, for garnishing

Melt the butter in a small nonstick skillet. Add the fennel and minced scallions and season lightly with salt and pepper. Cook over medium heat until just softened, stirring occasionally, about 3-5 minutes. Transfer to a large bowl and allow to cool slightly.

Add the sliced scallions, trout, dill, mayonnaise, lemon juice, and cream. Mix gently until well blended (see below left).

Bring a large pot of water to a boil. Salt to taste and add the pasta. Cook until just tender (check package directions for cooking times as this varies from brand to brand). Drain thoroughly and let cool.

Add the pasta to the vegetable and trout mixture and toss to coat evenly. Taste for seasoning. Serve the salad lightly chilled or at room temperature, garnished with dill, if desired.

VARIATION

IF PREFERRED, YOU CAN SUBSTITE SMOKED SALMON OR TUNA FOR THE TROUT.

TROUT AND BACON HASH

THIS GOURMET VERSION OF HASH MAKES A WONDERFUL BRUNCH DISH. SERVE IT WITH POACHED EGGS AND WHEAT TOAST ON THE SIDE.

SERVES 2

3 cups potatoes, cut in ½ inch cubes (3-4 medium-size potatoes)
salt and pepper
3 tablespoons unsalted butter
½ onion, minced
½ green bell pepper, seeded and minced
1 garlic clove, minced
2 ounces Canadian bacon, chopped
7 ounces skinless trout fillets, cut in ½ inch pieces
1 teaspoon dried oregano
1 tablespoon chopped fresh parsley (optional)

Put the potatoes in a saucepan, add cold water to cover, and bring to a boil. Add 1 tablespoon salt and simmer until just tender, 8-10 minutes. Drain and set the potatoes aside.

Melt 2 tablespoons of the butter in a large nonstick skillet. Add the onion, bell pepper, garlic, and bacon and cook over medium heat, stirring occasionally until the onion is just softened and golden in colour, about 5-8 minutes.

Add the remaining butter and the potatoes to the skillet. Cook over high heat, stirring occasionally, until the potatoes are lightly browned, about 5 minutes longer.

Add the trout, oregano, and parsley if using (see above). Season with salt and pepper. Continue cooking, smashing down with a wooden spatula, until the trout is cooked through, 3-4 minutes more. Serve immediately.

STUFFED POTATO SKINS

SPICING AND STUFFING GIVES THE CLASSIC BAKED POTATO A WHOLE NEW LIFE. THESE COMPLEMENT A ROAST CHICKEN OR BEEF BEAUTIFULLY, BUT ARE DELICIOUS SERVED SOLO AT LUNCH AS WELL.

SERVES 6

3 baking potatoes, about 12 ounces each, scrubbed and patted dry
1 tablespoon vegetable oil
3 tablespoons butter
1 onion, chopped
salt and pepper
1 green bell pepper, seeded and coarsely chopped
1 teaspoon paprika
1 cup shredded Monterey Jack or cheddar cheese.

Preheat the oven to 450°F.

Brush the potatoes all over with the oil. Prick them in several places on all sides with a fork.

Place in a baking dish. Bake until tender, about 1½ hours.

Meanwhile, heat the butter in a large nonstick skillet. Add the onion and a little salt and cook over medium heat until softened, about 5 minutes. Add the bell pepper and continue cooking until just tender but still crunchy, 2-3 minutes more. Stir in the paprika and set aside.

When the potatoes are done, halve them lengthwise. Scoop out the flesh, keeping the pieces coarse. Keep the potato skins warm.

Preheat the broiler.

Add the potato flesh to the skillet and cook over high heat, stirring, until the potato is lightly browned. Season with pepper.

Divide the vegetable mixture among the potato skins (see above).

Sprinkle the cheese on top. Broil until the cheese just melts, 3-5 minutes. Serve immediately.

VARIATION

FOR BACON-STUFFED POTATO SKINS, ADD ¾ CUP CHOPPED COOKED BACON TO THE COOKED POTATO FLESH AND VEGETABLES. STUFF AS ABOVE.

CAULIFLOWER AU GRATIN

THIS DELICATE VEGETABLE DISH PERFECTLY COMPLEMENTS CHICKEN, BEEF OR TURKEY ENTREES.

SERVES 4

2½ pounds cauliflower florets (about 1 large head)
3 tablespoons butter
3 tablespoons flour
2 cups milk
½ cup shredded sharp cheddar cheese
salt and pepper
3 bay leaves

Preheat the oven to 350°F. Grease a 12-inch round baking dish.

Bring a large pot of salted water to a boil. Add the cauliflower and cook until just tender but still firm, 7-8 minutes. Drain well.

Melt the butter in a heavy saucepan. Gradually whisk in the flour until thoroughly blended and cook until hot and bubbling. Gradually add the milk. Bring to a boil and continue cooking, stirring constantly, until thick.

Remove from the heat and stir in the shredded cheese. Season the sauce with salt and pepper to taste.

Place the bay leaves on the bottom of the prepared dish. Arrange the cauliflower florets on top in an even layer. Pour the cheese sauce evenly over the cauliflower.

Bake until browned, about 20-25 minutes. Serve immediately as side dish or tasty snack.

VARIATION

FOR A SAVORY VARIATION, SUBSTITUTE THE CHEDDAR WITH A SALTIER CHEESE, SUCH AS GRUYERE.

Wild Rice Pilaf

The crunchy, nutty taste of wild rice evokes the wide, windy marshes where it is harvested. It serves a few more when mixed with long grain rice — a boon because it is a luxury and luxuriously priced.

Serves 6

1 cup wild rice
salt and pepper
3 tablespoons butter
½ onion, minced
1 cup long-grain rice
2 cups chicken stock
⅔ cup sliced or slivered almonds
⅔ cup golden raisins
2 tablespoons chopped fresh parsley

Bring a large saucepan of water to a boil. Add the wild rice and 1 teaspoon salt. Cover and simmer gently until the rice is tender, 45-60 minutes. When done, drain well.

Meanwhile, melt 1 tablespoon of the butter in another saucepan. Add the onion and cook over medium heat until it is just softened, about 5 minutes. Stir in the long-grain rice and cook 1 minute more.

Stir in the stock and bring to a boil. Cover and simmer gently until the rice is tender and the liquid has been absorbed, about 30-40 minutes more.

Melt the remaining butter in a small skillet. Add the almonds and cook until they are just golden, 2-3 minutes, stirring occasionally. Set aside.

In a large bowl, combine the wild rice, long-grain rice, raisins, almonds, and parsley. Stir to mix. Taste and adjust the seasoning if necessary. Transfer to a warmed serving dish and serve immediately.

Winter Warmer
(Hot White Chocolate)

SERVE THIS ELEGANT VERSION OF THE CLASSIC AFTER A DAY'S HIKE IN THE MOUNTAINS.

SERVES 4

6 ounces white chocolate
1½ quarts milk
1 teaspoon coffee extract, or 2 teaspoons instant coffee powder
2 teaspoons orange-flavored liqueur (optional)

FOR SERVING

whipped cream
ground cinnamon or chocolate flakes

With a sharp knife, finely chop the white chocolate. (Try not to handle it too much or it will soften and stick together.)

Pour the milk into a medium-sized heavy saucepan and bring just to a boil (bubbles will form around the edge of the pan).

Add the chopped white chocolate, coffee extract or powder, and orange-flavored liqueur if using. Stir until the chocolate has melted.

Divide the hot chocolate among 4 coffee mugs. Top each with a rosette or spoonful of whipped cream and a sprinkling of ground cinnamon or chocolate flakes if preferred.

Serve immediately while piping hot.

Easy Hazelnut Fudge

HAZELNUTS AND CHOCOLATE HAVE ALWAYS MARRIED WELL. THIS FUDGE IS IRRESISTIBLE.

MAKES 16 SQUARES

⅔ cup evaporated milk
1¾ cups sugar
⅛ teaspoon salt
½ cup halved hazelnuts
2 cups semisweet chocolate chips
1 teaspoon hazelnut liqueur (optional)

Grease an 8-inch square cake pan. Combine the milk, sugar, and salt in a heavy saucepan. Bring to a boil over medium heat, stirring constantly. Simmer, stirring, 5 minutes.

Remove from the heat and add the hazelnuts, chocolate chips, and liqueur if using. Stir until the chocolate has completely melted.

Quickly pour the fudge mixture into the prepared pan and spread it out evenly. Let cool.

When set, cut into 1-inch squares. Store in an airtight container, separated by layers of wax paper.

VARIATION

FOR EASY PEANUT BUTTER FUDGE, SUBSTITUTE PEANUT BUTTER CHIPS FOR THE CHOCOLATE CHIPS AND REPLACE THE HAZELNUTS WITH PEANUTS.

Northwestern Brown Betty

Pears, dried cherries and hazelnuts give this traditional dessert a distinctive new taste. A scoop of vanilla frozen yogurt makes it taste even better.

Serves 6

2¼ pounds pears (about 8)
¼ cup lemon juice
3 cups fresh bread crumbs, preferably from egg bread.
6 tablespoons butter, melted
⅔ cup dried cherries
⅔ cup coarsely chopped hazelnuts
½ cup brown sugar, firmly packed
1-2 tablespoons butter, cut in small pieces
whipped cream, for serving

Preheat the oven to 375°F. Grease an 8-inch square cake pan.

Peel, core, and dice the pears. Sprinkle them with the lemon juice to prevent discoloration.

Combine the bread crumbs and melted butter in a bowl. Spread a scant one-third of the crumb mixture on the bottom of the prepared dish.

Top with half of the pears. Sprinkle over half of the dried cherries, half of the hazelnuts, and half of the sugar. Repeat the layers, then finish with a layer of crumbs.

Dot with pieces of butter (see left). Bake until golden, 30-35 minutes. Serve hot, with whipped cream.

Cook's Tip

Choose your pears carefully. They should be firm to the touch but yielding slightly at the stalk end. Ensure the stalks are still attached.

Rhubarb-Strawberry Crisp

IF YOU SNEAKILY DOUBLE THE RECIPE FOR THIS CLASSIC SWEET TART DESSERT, YOU'LL BE SURE TO HAVE LEFTOVERS FOR BREAKFAST.

SERVES 4

8 ounces strawberries, hulled
1 pound rhubarb, diced
½ cup granulated sugar
1 tablespoon cornstarch
⅓ cup fresh orange juice
1 cup flour
1 cup rolled oats
½ cup light brown sugar, firmly packed
½ teaspoon ground cinnamon
½ cup ground almonds
10 tablespoons (1¼ sticks) cold butter
1 egg, lightly beaten

Preheat the oven to 350°F.

If the strawberries are large, cut them in half. Combine the strawberries, rhubarb, and granulated sugar in a 2-quart baking dish (see right).

In a small bowl, blend the cornstarch with the orange juice. Pour this mixture over the fruit and stir gently to coat. Set the baking dish aside while making the topping.

In a bowl, toss together the flour, oats, brown sugar, cinnamon, and almonds. With a pastry blender or 2 knives, cut in the chilled butter until the mixture resembles coarse crumbs, about 10 minutes. Stir in the beaten egg.

Spoon the oat mixture evenly over the fruit and press down gently. Bake until browned, 50-60 minutes. Serve the crisp warm.

Blackberry Cobbler

If you go out in the woods to pick blackberries for this mouth-watering dessert, keep an eye out for hungry bears. They love berries as much as we do.

Serves 8

6 cups blackberries (about 1¾ pounds)
1 cup sugar
3 tablespoons flour
grated rind of 1 lemon
2 tablespoons sugar mixed with ¼ teaspoon grated nutmeg

For the topping

2 cups flour
1 cup sugar
1 tablespoon baking powder
⅛ teaspoon salt
1 cup milk
½ cup (1 stick) butter, melted

Preheat the oven to 350°F.

In a bowl, combine the blackberries, sugar, flour, and lemon rind. Stir gently to blend. Transfer to a 2-quart baking dish.

For the topping sift the flour, sugar, baking powder, and salt into a large bowl. Set aside. In a large measure, combine the milk and butter.

Gradually stir the milk mixture into the dry ingredients and stir until the batter is just smooth.

Spoon the batter over the berries, spreading to the edges (see above).

Sprinkle the surface with the sugar-nutmeg mixture. Bake until the batter topping is set and lightly browned, about 50 minutes. Serve hot.

Cook's Tip

If picking your own blackberries, be sure to use small containers as this delicate fruit can be easily crushed by its own weight. Discard any damaged, moldy or green berries and remove any remaining stalks. Wash thoroughly.

Baked Apples

DRIED APRICOTS GIVE THIS HOMELY DESSERT A RICH TART FLAVOR. OTHER DRIED FRUITS MAY ALSO BE USED TO STUFF THE APPLES: PEARS, RAISINS OR DRIED CRANBERRIES, FOR EXAMPLE.

SERVES 6

½ cup chopped dried apricots
½ cup chopped walnuts
1 teaspoon grated lemon rind
¼ teaspoon ground cinnamon
½ cup light brown sugar, firmly packed
2 tablespoons butter, at room temperature
6 baking apples
1 tablespoon melted butter

Preheat the oven to 375°F.

In a bowl, combine the apricots, walnuts, lemon rind, and cinnamon. Add the sugar and butter and stir until thoroughly combined.

Core the apples, without cutting all the way through to the base (see above right). With a small knife, widen the top of each opening by about 1½ inches to make room for the filling.

Spoon the apricot and walnut filling into each opening in the apples, making sure to pack it down tightly.

Place the apples in a baking dish just large enough to hold them comfortably side by side.

Brush the apples with the melted butter. Bake until they are tender, 40-45 minutes. Serve hot.

COOK'S TIP

TO CORE AN APPLE, FIRST WASH THE APPLE, LEAVING THE SKIN ON. PUSH DOWN THE CENTER WITH AN APPLE CORER ALMOST TO THE BASE. PULL THE CYLINDER UP AND REMOVE THE CORE AND SEEDS.

Blueberry-Hazelnut Cheesecake

Berries add color and tartness to the rich creamy taste of classic cheesecake. It can be prepared one day in advance, but add the fruit just before serving.

Serves 6-8

12 ounces blueberries
1 tablespoon honey
6 tablespoons granulated sugar
1 teaspoon plus 1 tablespoon fresh lemon juice
6 ounces cream cheese, at room temperature
1 egg
1 teaspoon hazelnut liqueur (optional)
½ cup whipping cream

For the crust

1⅔ cups ground hazelnuts
⅔ cup flour
⅛ teaspoon salt
4 tablespoons butter, at room temperature
⅓ cup light brown sugar, firmly packed
1 egg yolk

For the crust, put the hazelnuts in a large bowl. Sift in the flour and salt, and stir to mix. Set aside.

Beat the butter with the brown sugar until light and fluffy. Beat in the egg yolk. Gradually fold in the nut mixture, in 3 batches.

Press the dough into a greased 9-inch pie pan, spreading it evenly. Form a rim around the top edge slightly thicker than the sides. Cover and refrigerate at least 30 minutes.

Preheat oven to 350°F.

Meanwhile, for the topping, combine the blueberries, honey, 1 tablespoon of the granulated sugar, and 1 teaspoon lemon juice in a heavy saucepan. Cook the mixture over low heat, stirring occasionally, until the berries have given off some liquid but still retain their shape, 5-7 minutes. Remove from the heat and set aside.

Place the crust in the oven and bake 15 minutes. Remove and let cool while making the filling.

Beat together the cream cheese and remaining granulated sugar until light and fluffy. Add the egg, remaining lemon juice, the liqueur, if using, and the cream and beat until thoroughly incorporated.

Pour the cheese mixture into the crust and spread evenly. Bake until just set, 20-25 minutes.

Let the cheesecake cool completely on a wire rack, then cover and refrigerate at least 1 hour.

Spread the blueberry mixture evenly over the top of the cheesecake. Serve at cool room temperature.

Baked Peaches with Raspberry Sauce

THIS BRILLIANTLY-COLORED DESSERT SHOULD BE SERVED IN SUMMER WHEN PEACHES AND RASPBERRIES ARE AT THEIR PEAK.

SERVES 6

3 tablespoons unsalted butter, at room temperature

¼ cup sugar

1 egg, beaten

¼ cup ground almonds

6 ripe peaches

FOR THE SAUCE

1 cup raspberries

1 tablespoon confectioners' sugar

1 tablespoon fruit-flavored brandy (optional)

Preheat the oven to 350°F.

Beat the butter with the sugar until soft and fluffy. Beat in the egg. Add the ground almonds and beat just to blend well together.

Halve the peaches and remove the pits. With a spoon, scrape out some of the flesh from each peach half, slightly enlarging the hollow left by the pit. Reserve the excess peach flesh to use in the sauce.

Place the peach halves on a baking sheet (it may be necessary, to secure the peaches with crumpled foil to keep them from falling over). Completely fill in the hollow of each peach half with the almond mixture.

Place in the oven and bake until the almond filling is puffed and golden and the peaches are very tender, about 30 minutes.

Meanwhile, for the sauce, combine the raspberries, confectioner's sugar and brandy, if using, in a food processor or blender. Add the reserved peach flesh. Process until smooth. Press through a strainer set over a bowl to remove fibers and seeds.

Let the peaches cool slightly. Place 2 peach halves on each plate and spoon some of the sauce over each peach.

Serve immediately while still hot.

INDEX